The Ghosts of Newgrange

Ancient Ceremony Remembered

By: Kate Bowditch

www.lulu.com

TITLE: The Ghosts of Newgrange; Ancient Ceremony Remembered
     Kate Bowditch

Edited by Sophie Horste and Sharon Danford
Graphic design and illustrations by the author
Published by Lulu at: www.lulu.com

ISBN: 978-1-257-92856-9

Also by **Kate Bowditch**:

20-20 Insight, Advanced Theory and Practice of Hypnosis, 2008

The Mountain and the Shadow, A Pagan's Journey Into Death, 2010

Both available at: **www.lulu.com**

Table of Contents

Acknowledgments   4

Explanation   5

Foreword   7

Song for Newgrange   9

Bru na Boinne   10

Mists of History   11

The Life Cycle of Ceremony   16

2003: The Beginning   20

  The First Visit to Newgrange   21

  It Began Here   23

  The Journal   31

  The Question   48

  The Journal Continues   49

2006: Second Visit to Newgrange   57

2008: The Ending   64

  Finishing the Work   65

  The Leave-taking   67

Conclusions   70

  Putting It All Together   71

  Reconstructing Beliefs and Ceremonies   74

  Healing   79

  The Healing at Newgrange   81

PHOTOGRAPHS: 27-30

Sidebars: Reiki and Alpha-Reiki 26, What is a Moon Ceremony? 38

STORY: "The Shaman of Newgrange"   82

APPENDIX, Pg. 91: Hypnosis and Hypnotic Inductions 92, The Safe Place 93, What is the Past Life Experience? 94, Two Rings of Stone 96, The Tarot 99

Bibliography   100

*****

Acknowledgements

There are those who support and carry us. Sometimes we are unaware of this, due to our own focus. Sometimes they are unaware of what they've done, not realizing the impact of their gifts. Nonetheless, this book could not have been completed without the following folks, whom I love and give gratitude to:

My daughter Jessica, who stood with me through some of the low places, quietly saying
"Yes, you can do this."

My friends: Sophie Horste, editor, ever with the gentle nudge
Sharon Danford, editor, author, encourager
Stephen Tuell, for his necessary skepticism and encouragement

My sisters Elise and Sabra, who, in their very different roles, gave me encouragement and validation

My husband Vernon McCoy, for his unwavering love of Ireland, and his utter belief in the experiences he was having and their meaning

All those who shared our burden in the last days of Vernon's life

***

To paraphrase David, a wise man I know:

"Making ceremonies came before a lot of knowledge about the universe. To think as they did, you have to go to 'the drum-circle in your heart' that exists behind logic and behind science."

May we all, at least once in our lives, hear our own heart's drum-circle and pay attention.

*****

Explanation

The book in your hand is in no way a scholarly treatise weaving history from scattered temple stones and shelved books in libraries. Rather it results from paying attention to an unusual man's awakening to his own ancient memory.

I am a trained hypnotherapist. I help my clients allow themselves free access to their memories while in a deeply relaxed state. These memories are then gleaned for misunderstandings which have continued to play out in their lives. Often clients can remember positive moments from their past that were forgotten for one reason or another. In either case, clients can apply the new information to their lives for their benefit.

In some cases, we can go further back into the memory, before infancy, before birth, and into what is experienced as a moment in a life that existed before this person's current life. This is called a "Past Life Experience." The acceptance of Past Life Experience is embedded in the belief that the human soul is ageless, living again and again in this world in order to have experiences needed to learn lessons. This belief holds that major unresolved issues are faced in repeated lifetimes until they are resolved. Sometimes calling forth a Past Life Experience can help resolve such an issue, freeing the person to enjoy their current life more fully.

This book is the result of trusting and following my husband when he made a spontaneous "jump" to a past life. He was a gentle and an aware man, though not one to give much thought to hypnosis or memory examination. And yet he had such an experience. His memories have permitted an imperfect yet exciting view into the minds and customs of the people of Ireland, at Newgrange, thousands of years ago.

Welcome, dear Reader. Come. Explore the possibilities of just who those people may have been, and of what Newgrange may have meant to them.

*****

<u>Foreword</u>

Perhaps you will read this foreword before turning the pages to get to the rest of the story. You may wonder a moment why this book is in your hands. Perhaps it will be something about remembering…some soft, far-away filament of a memory you can't quite name, or even believe is there.

The chasing of just such filaments has been the business of much of my work as a clinical hypnotherapist. This filament, this un-nameable feeling of knowing something that makes no "sense" in your everyday world, can influence how you move through your world, and is available to you in its fullness only in the place and time of deep trance. One such use of trance, when gently guided, and without direct coaching, is called the Past Life Experience. There are many who believe that within this experience, you can see and feel (sometimes hear and smell) the surroundings that your soul experienced long before you came to the life you are now living.

Much has been written about the Past Life Experience, which forms an important part of my clinical practice. When my husband spontaneously began experiencing himself in a different time and body at a place called Newgrange outside Dublin, Ireland, I began documenting what was happening. I knew immediately that it was important to do this.

This book is about this man's following of those filaments of his deepest memory back to the physical location of their beginnings. This was at Newgrange, an ancient site of powerful though indistinct purpose. The record of those memories sheds light upon what the spiritual beliefs and ancient ceremonies could have been for the people there at that time. Vernon's travels back into his memory breathe life into the stones and lintels of that structure and reveal some of their deep secrets.

The writing of this book is the result of recording my husband's unexpected "revisiting" Newgrange as it existed some thousands of years ago. With my help, he chased those memories deep within him, experiencing the ceremonies as they existed then. From the work we did together we came to understand Newgrange in a new way. We now see that Newgrange awaits us. It awaits us all. It awaits our awakening to an awareness of its true nature: Newgrange is the present day spiritual focal point for the community of us who are of Northern European decent and who keep the Earth at the center of our spiritual lives. Other locations may hold the same meaning for those whose ancestors walked a different land, but Newgrange is our home, our Center, our Mother. It (She) is our place of pilgrimage, our touchstone to the amazing power accessible to us all through intent, balance, and love. Perhaps you, too, can begin to remember the earliest days of these ancestors as you read this book.

KB

*****

Song For Newgrange

The ancient words and
The ancient ceremonies
Have gone;
Scattered to the winds
By time, force, and neglect.

Yielding, people walked a different path.

Ancient energy
Awakens our memory.
Be still.
We need to listen
With all our heart and soul.

Stones call us home, whispering our names.

The ancient stones and
The ancient ceremonies
Call us.
We awaken now,
Remembering our names.

Heads turn, hearts opening to the sound.

We sing old lessons.
We sing with a new language.
We laugh!
We dance new rhythms.
Living ceremony!

Returning Home, walking straight again.

Kate Bowditch

*****

Bru na Boinne

Since its restoration in the 1970's Newgrange has become a major tourist attraction in Ireland. It sits as part of the largest and one of the most important prehistoric megalithic sites in Europe. Buses to the site arrive in a steady rhythm throughout the day. Groups of visitors are led through its narrow entry and lectures are given deep inside, noting the roof construction, the designs in the stones, and the "burial chambers" off the sides of the central hall.

When going there, the visitor first arrives at an excellent interpretive museum called the Bru na Boinne Visitors Center. This is not a museum of glass cases, but a wonderful hall of interactive and exciting information. The displays are extensive and the visitor gets a deep experience of the Mound. You will learn about its history, its use as an astronomical time keeper, and its construction. There is no hint left, however, of the nature of the ceremony there, or how the people thought about life and death. What did they think when they looked up at the cosmos itself? Those ideas vanished with the people themselves. We are left to wonder as we touch the stones they touched, standing in the chamber they built. Who were they?

Many are satisfied enough to forgo the bus ride and the long walk required to get to Newgrange itself. The Visitors Center, and the Mound for some, are certainly a "must do" for anyone visiting Dublin. Buses to the site are available at the Irish Tourist Bureau in Dublin.

*****

Mists of History

Mist rises slowly from the Boyne River, coaxed by dawn's arrival. Gently, silently, the mist surrenders the river, revealing its deep green banks and sodden livestock hunkering in the grass. It creeps along the hillsides, returning the houses and barns to view, returning the trees. Finally, softly, the immense strange bulk of Newgrange emerges, nestled into the top of the hill.

Newgrange greets the visitor silently, hoarding its ancient secrets. The brilliant white stone face shines back at the tentative dawn, beckoning the viewer to enter the blackness within.

Newgrange came into being some five thousand years ago, as a now long-vanished people hauled and stacked enormous stone slabs from distant places to build its walls. They then lay more great stones flat in ever-smaller layers of circles to create a high roof over a central chamber below. The roof stones were so neatly and tightly placed that no rainfall has entered the chamber in some 5,000 years. The exception was a small trickle that was deliberately directed towards the large stone bowl in the right-hand alcove. This was possibly for star viewing or "skrying," a form of fortune telling with water. This trickle has stopped as the restoration included top protection.

The Mound was built of stone and sod, with occasional clay "mortar" as a binding agent. Some 200,000 tons of stone make its structure. An estimated 1,600 granite boulders were used in the construction of Newgrange. Ninety-seven enormous and beautifully carved stones ring the mound, retaining the massive downward/outward pressure of the stone and sod above. There is no evidence of the method the people   used to transport these massive stones from their distant quarries in the Wicklow Mountains. Some estimate that it took eighty men four days to haul one stone just a mile or two. We can understand, therefore, why the construction of Newgrange is estimated to have lasted for over 70 years.

Newgrange has overlooked the River Boyne for some five thousand years. It was in place before the building of either Stonehenge in England or the Great Pyramid of Egypt. Those who built Newgrange had come and gone by then, taking the purpose of the structure, and their ceremonies, with them.

Only one entrance to Newgrange beckons the visitor. This sole entrance opens to a passage just over 60 feet in length. The passage is so narrow that the visitor must proceed hunched and crowded, turning sideways to get through. It is so low as to keep the visitor humble throughout the entry. Deep inside, the visitor enters a central chamber big enough for ten or more people to stand upright. Three low recesses adorn the walls. There is one large stone basin in each recess, their ancient purpose unknown. The ceiling over the central chamber is high, and the visitor easily stands, grateful for the headroom after the difficult entry.

The Mound of Newgrange is massive, almost the size of a football field. People on the walkway towards its entrance become mere dots of color in the photographs they take. Three stones, the central one the size of an SUV and carved with wonderful swirling spirals, cross the entrance. (To allow the visitors to get into and out of Newgrange without having to climb over the stones, the park personnel have built two stairways up and over this barricade. See Pg: 27) These stones were placed there much later than the mound's construction for reasons unknown. Beyond these stones, in the grass before the entrance, an arc of rough-hewn stones stand upright, forming a vanguard. These were placed there some thousand years after Newgrange was built, again for reasons unknown.

In ancient legends, Aonghus was chieftain of the mythical people known as the Tuatha Dé Danann. These were the race of the other-world peoples who resided at Brú na Bóinne, the land along the river where Newgrange was built. Aongus' father was the Dagdha, the 'Good God', and a principal deity of the Tuatha Dé Danann. His mother was Bóinn, or Boann, the goddess of the River Boyne. Newgrange was built in a powerful place, home to powerful families.

Newgrange has been described as a burial mound (or passage tomb), a place for ceremony, a solar calendar, and a temple. The solar and lunar functions there are not disputed due to the wonderful archaeological and mathematical work done to understand its careful layout and construction. However, if it was a burial mound, the bones of the dead do not exist to tell us their stories. There are no telltale graves, no piles of bones, no skulls decorating walls or crevices—not even in carvings. When Newgrange was first discovered in 1699, the remains of only three more recent bodies were found. Details of the mound's connection to the dead and any hint of the ceremonies performed there have vanished with those who lived and breathed there. Only some of the heroes remain in legends and myths. Who were these people? How did they mourn their dead? How did they celebrate marriages? How did they arrange their trades with one another? What did they fear? What relationship did they have with the cosmos? The answers to these questions were not made of stone, and have vanished as they themselves have vanished.

The Mound is perfectly aligned with the horizon and with the location of sunrise at the Winter Solstice. Inside, the passageway itself rises, to mimic the rise of the hill on which it stands, so that a person entering at the mouth below is at the top of the hill when reaching the center, deep within the Mound. This perfect interior rising allows the rays of the Solstice sunrise to enter the mound through the light box (or window) above the entry door, and touch the ground at the Mound's very center for about 20 minutes. The center is illuminated in this way for only five days. This is at the Winter Solstice, the coldest, bleakest time of year. Inside the chamber the stone slabs shine so brightly in the reflected Solstice light that one can see easily. Then the sun moves on. Throughout the year, from the days just past winter Solstice to the days just prior to it, the mound is utterly dark. Newgrange has welcomed the Solstice dawn for so long that the earth has shifted in its position in the cosmos, causing the light to enter slightly to the side of center. The Solstice light is now recreated electrically for the visitors' experience.

Newgrange was not alone as a ceremonial mound in the Pagan world. Mounded chambers and burial centers dot the European landscape from Scotland down through central Europe. Knowth is home to several smaller mounds, and can easily be part of a tour to Newgrange. Lough Crew maintains its vigil from its mountaintop nearby. There is a little one at Ireland's Hill of Tara. The

14

entry to Maes Howe peeks from a hillside in the Orkneys, off the northeastern coast of Scotland. Countless numbers lie untouched, inaccessible, or unknown throughout the countryside of Scotland, Ireland, England and northern Europe. together.

Newgrange, however, is wonderfully restored and accessible. It was rebuilt with the stones found around its crumbled base, giving it a brilliant white facade with a black stone entrance. It is accessible by a narrow blacktop path along its side. Its reconstruction is more an interpretation of the earlier appearance than a restoration, and there was much controversy over just how to do this work. The re-builders took the bold path. Whereas most of the other known mounds now hunker into a hillside, blending with the landscape, Newgrange stands proudly announcing her presence to all.

"She" was huge by the standards of her day, and received the people's ceremony as the sacred center of their known world. She calls to us again now to return, to touch her stones, to enter her chamber and stand within her flanks. We can open our hearts and minds to her and step inside with a new understanding of her purpose.

Newgrange stands before the earth-centered dawn. She is our first great temple, our first and last Great Ceremonial Home. Perhaps we can gather before her now in love and gratitude, and with deep reverence for the earth and the cosmos

*****

The Life Cycle of Ceremony

"Ceremony." The word itself conjures images of mystery and a little magic. Robes perhaps, certainly colors. We envision actions that are different from the everyday things we do. We may dress differently, keep talk to a minimum, or sit in ways that are different. We try not to let our attention wander. Ceremony is set aside in time and place. It is held in a special building, or in a prepared place outside, on a special day, or special time of day. In ceremony people have roles that may differ from their everyday behavior. There is a creative use of silence and sound. Sometimes there is singing or chanting. Instruments, from simple sticks to violins and pipe organs, enhance the total effect.

In ceremony an environment is created that is separate in time, location, behavior, sound, and/or intent. This environment surrounds and holds all participants in a state of suspension while certain "work" occurs. Every known culture uses ceremony for specific "work" which, by the ceremony itself, becomes sacred. This "work" may be to celebrate births or graduations, for healings, or to express gratitude. It can be for coming-of-age, to ask animals to offer themselves to the hunters, for joining couples, or for safe-passage. It may be a funeral. Ceremony is also for small, intimate moments, attended by just one or two people.

In general people enter a ceremony expecting something to happen to themselves as well as to a targeted person, group or object. In a wedding ceremony, for example, two single people are joined to become a couple—and all in the wedding party are expected to behave slightly differently towards them from that time onward. In a coming-of-age ceremony, the participants bid farewell to the child and welcome a young adult. This is why many ceremonial occasions are, in one form or another, "invitation only." A neutral observer, unfamiliar with the participants or the nature of the ceremony, creates a "dead spot," a place where the energy of the ceremony seems to go flat, thus weakening the effect of the whole.

Ceremony is very much a part of life in all cultures and takes many forms. The details may change from group to group, or even from family to family. There is a main flavor to any ceremony that clings, however, and can be quite specific. One example is the American Thanksgiving Dinner. Basically, it's a meal. It involves people sitting at a somewhat formalized table to eat. Maybe it's turkey, or goose, or ham—or chicken or fish. It is, however, a special meal, eaten with the intent of expressing gratitude for life's bounty.

Essential weddings involve seeing two individuals come together to proclaim their new relationship. A ceremony itself breathes only with the life that the members put into it: the colors, the food, the music, who sits where, how long it lasts, and who does what function. In many cases these details are not written down, but are passed from parent to child. Sometimes they are simply absorbed by people through participation as time goes by. These details become "the way we do this" and are carried forward in time.

Sometimes, however, ceremonies die. Their people may wander so far from the physical center of the ceremony that it loses its power, becoming neglected and forgotten. Often new ways of thinking make an old ceremony feel obsolete, and so it is discarded. On the other hand, a conquering people can forbid the ceremonies of the conquered or change them so profoundly that they become unrecognizable. Within a few generations even the memories of the original ceremonies are gone. Their shadows remain as tales of the past, holding heroes or magical lands. If not understood, honored and nourished, the details and the life of ceremonies dissipate like mist to vanish in the light of the new day.

When ceremonies are forcibly removed from a culture, the thread of desire can remain in the fabric of a people. The need is still felt as an unquenched yearning. Given a moment of peace to reflect and remember, people will reignite that yearning and rebuild their ceremony. The upwelling of this remembering and rebuilding of ceremony among the First Peoples in the United States is testament to this. So, too, is the reawakening of religious practice in what was once the USSR.

In one of these ways, the ceremonial practices of Newgrange were lost. Where the people went, and just why, is also lost. Only the stones remain to tell us that something went on there. Something went on that was so important and consuming that a stone-age people would spend years hauling massive stones from distant quarries to build Newgrange and smaller structures like it. They did not live in these structures. Nor did they store food in them. These structures were decorated with ceremonial carvings. That we know. Just what were the ceremonies that took place there? What did they look like? What were the sounds? Who did what? How long did they last? What were the purposes of these ceremonies? There must have been more than one ceremony held at Newgrange to justify the building of such a structure. What were the details? These have been lost and barely speculated upon.

In a strange series of events, recorded here as they occurred, one person has remembered. One person courageously pursued the threads of his memory through deep time and distant place. He was able to recall and record forgotten details from that time so long ago. He was able to remember bits and pieces of the people's ways there at Newgrange. He paid attention, returning to them in memory, hearing them and seeing their ceremony. He came to understand that something had gone very wrong there long, long ago. He understood that there was something important that still played out in the purpose and power of Newgrange. And so he set about to right that wrong, and to help people understand in greater detail what Newgrange was. He breathed refreshing life back into its ceremony.

This book and the lessons within it are his gift to his beloved Ireland, and to all who love the earth and walk in a sacred manner.

*****

2003

The Beginning

*****

The First Visit to Newgrange

2003

In the spring of 2003, my husband Vernon and I joined my sister and her husband on a long vacation to Ireland, Scotland, and England. While in Ireland, we all took one of those tour buses from Dublin to Newgrange. We greatly enjoyed the Visitors Center and decided to tackle the Mound. This required a bus ride from the far side of the river near the Visitors Center through the countryside to the base of the hill supporting Newgrange. From there it was a short walk to a viewing house where we got a lecture about what we were about to see. Then came the long walk up the hill.

Following the walkway, we did not approach Newgrange head-on. Rather, we came upon its flank; its imposing white walls confronting our curiosity with silence. Newgrange appeared to grow as we approached. Walking up the hill to its base, I suppressed a desire to place my hand on one of the stones in the wall, the way I would stroke the belly of a huge horse, or perhaps an elephant, or whale. The walkway was just far enough away from the structure to inhibit me. The immensity of it all invited me to walk its perimeter, again suppressed as the tour group moved ahead. As we neared the end of the walk-way we saw the huge standing stones protecting the front, and succumbed to their invitation to stay at the front of the Mound.

We finally joined a smallish crowd that entered the mound. We stood shoulder to shoulder with them inside. The guide spoke of its history and of how it was built.

She told us that the stones across the entry and the standing stones in front of the mound had been placed there about a thousand years after the mound was built. She said the mound had been abandoned. It was later reused by others who put the stones there. She did not say why. I was quite taken by Newgrange and comfortable inside the Mound. I saw the obvious correlation of it to a womb and birth canal. (There is an old Irish word - Brú - which means "womb"). The likeness to a birth canal is detailed, even to the need to shove one shoulder at a time through the space between the stones to get out. Vernon was interested in its architecture but, being a bit of a claustrophobe, he was more focused on the outside. The idea of being in a tomb for very long left him, well, cold.

Our trip continued, with visits to other wonderful Irish sites of history, of other places with stones and ancient walls. We went to Scotland, continuing up to the Orkney Islands to visit The Ring of Brodgar (Pg.25, 81), down through Edinburgh, and into England. Our photo album is thick with prints, and our lives greatly enriched by the experiences we had. I was unprepared for what was about to occur to us in the next few years...

*****

It Began Here

2004

About a year after we returned home from our trip, Vernon had a stroke while we were in a store. He was able to continue standing, and did not tell me, or anyone else, that something was wrong. His speech was not affected and it was only when I noticed inconsistencies in his movements that we went to the hospital.

The effects of Vernon's stroke appeared minimal to the outsider. Inside, however, he became frustrated at being unable to do things requiring fine motor skills, and he would get disoriented when out in public. This made him very anxious, and he became resistant to going to rehab. He and I decided to do some Alpha-Reiki at home to help calm him. (Pg.26)

A series of unusual events unfolded as we began regular Alpha-Reiki sessions with him. I am a therapist myself, so I keep records. Out of habit, I recorded the events as they occurred. (For further clarification of some terms and concepts, see the Appendix, Pg. 91)

During the first Alpha-Reiki treatment after his stroke, while he was calm and deeply quiet, Vernon made a spontaneous mental "jump" to a Past Life Experience. The "jump" was "spontaneous" because I had given him no guidance to do anything. I had only given him suggestions to visit his previously well-established "Safe Place," which in his mind is a park-like setting with a little fountain and a bench in it, to find peace and calm. We had had no recent discussion of Newgrange, or Ireland, or travel of any kind.

In the "jump" he had experienced himself at this ancient, sacred place called Newgrange. Upon awakening, Vernon stated simply, "We're going back to Ireland." He was able to remember the details of his experience, which I recorded. He also wanted to continue this work with the Alpha-Reiki, which he felt benefited him. I continued as his guide, and over the next two years he "traveled" several times to Newgrange while in the trance state. He did this spontaneously during Alpha-Reiki sessions and by direct suggestion while in hypnosis.

During these past life "travels," he had no control over the time or place he visited, and so experienced Newgrange during different times in its history, and to my surprise, experienced the lives of different people who were there. The importance of his experiencing Newgrange in this way became clear as we worked. He slowly revealed the main ceremonial purpose of Newgrange, some details of the ceremonies, and a critical moment in its history. That he was experiencing Newgrange, rather than the many other places we had visited while we were there, was interesting to me because of his initial vague disinterest in the mound itself.

Although he loved to read about history, neither Vernon nor I read books about Newgrange, its history, structure or mythology. We chose not to infuse the spontaneous "memories" with known data.

As we worked, however, the reasons for his focus there became clear. Another trip to the mound itself in real time became irresistible. In the spring of 2006 we took a second trip to Ireland. To reduce Vernon's discomfort when in unfamiliar surroundings, we stayed in Dublin, taking day trips out to sites and returning to the same B&B at night. We went to visit Newgrange in particular. He was able to stand in the exact place at the site where he felt he needed to be to "complete the story." He was able to accomplish an important task for Ireland, for Newgrange, and for himself, a task that had been interrupted so very long ago.

*****

Reiki and Alpha-Reiki

Reiki is the name of a fast growing, yet still esoteric form of energy healing. It is believed that by focusing the energy of the Universe, called Ki or Chi (life force), through their own body, the trained Reiki healer can direct this energy into the body of a client. This directed energy adds to the client's own diffuse acceptance of the energy available in the environment, allowing for internal healing of a physical and emotional nature.

Reiki can be used to alleviate aches and pains, for post surgery healing, and for healing of many other specific conditions and situations---always *after* full medical attention has been given.

Reiki is a healing modality that is useful for one-self, and can be used for animals as well. The energy is directed through the hands of the healer, held over the affected areas of the client, who is lying down. Some Reiki healers place their hands directly upon the body (with permission of the client) while others do not, holding their hands about 1"- 2" over the client. Both methods are acceptable. Usually the client is prone on a massage table, fully clothed, and relaxed.

This author is a mental health counselor and hypnotherapist, and trained in Reiki to the Third Degree. Naturally, I am curious about what is actually going on inside the client during Reiki treatment. I begin the Reiki session with my client in a light hypnotic trance state. Helping them visualize both their interior landscape, and the energy itself, allows them to directly experience the healing. They can also "see" where blocks to healing exist and what those blocks look like. We remove those blocks together through visualization, producing faster and deeper healing.

I call this process Alpha-Reiki.

Approaching Newgrange today

The face of Newgrange

Vernon and standing stone in front of Newgrange

The Spiral Stone in front of the door

The Ring of Brodgar, Isle of Orkney, Scotland

Vernon and the author at Newgrange 2006

Newgrange before the Guardian Stones were placed (artist's view)

Vernon taking pictures at the face of Newgrange

The Journal

2005-2006

The following is from the journal I kept of Vernon's trance experiences as they occurred:

02/05   (This occurred during a regular Alpha-Reiki treatment we did after his stroke.)

During an Alpha-Reiki treatment with colleague Sophie Horste, Vernon became immensely sad, but continued with the work. This is what he described after the session:

He was standing outside the great chambered mound we now call Newgrange, near what is now Dublin. The standing stones and the carved stone at the opening were not there. He was there, he said, at the time *"when the Mound was understood and was central to the people."* The Old Shaman was dead and his body had been placed inside the Mound. All the people were gathered around for the ceremony marking his end. The time was the Solstice and the Shaman's body had been held for this ceremonial day. Vernon understood that the people believed that the Winter Solstice was the only morning in the year when a person's soul could be freed from the body and from this earth. He reported what he had experienced:

It had been a good year. Old Shaman's body was the only one in the Mound this day. Vernon experienced himself as the new Shaman for the community. He could see the people, and he could see what he called "The Shadow People", or "The Ghosts." They were gray apparitions of all those people of the mound who had died before in their history. They filled the valley behind him, behind the living people. All were there for the Old Shaman's passage.

As the Solstice sun rose on this day it pierced the "light box", or window, of the Mound. The rising sun's light flooded the box, illuminating the dry stones of the Mound's interior. The Shaman's soul lifted from the body then and rode the shaft of the Solstice light out through the box, free. Vernon, as the New Shaman, only then understood he was both the Old Shaman and the New Shaman, for they had somehow become one.

02/05

Vernon got a short flash of Newgrange later in another session. He was in trance, walking to his "Safe Place" that he visits on occasion. It has a view of a forest, and this time the forest opened to reveal Newgrange. Again, it was before the great stones were placed in front of it. In his view, only the Shadow People were there. He knew, somehow, that they were waiting. Waiting for what?

03/21/05

We were both on treadmills at our local health club, walking nowhere. Vernon had a far-away look in his eye. I was watching Funny Videos that were inane enough to keep me walking. Here is what Vernon reported he saw:

"I was walking the long, dry, dusty road up to the ancient Medicine Wheel in northern Wyoming. As I reached the top of the hill I walked into Newgrange instead. It was all there: the green grass, soft air, and the white stones of the outer wall. The great carved stone lay across the entrance as it does today. A group of Shadow People stood off to one side. They were the same ones from before. Together they sent me a strong message: "We are waiting." I was surprised. Waiting for what?" (See: Big Horn Medicine Wheel, Pg. 97)

3/26/05

My friend, Sophie, and I gave him another Alpha-Reiki treatment. Vernon went again to Newgrange and learned more about it and his role there. Interestingly, he didn't "come back" after the treatment. He remained unfocussed and pale. Sophie suggested sending him back to finish his work, which I did. He finished the work, and this time came back with good color and focus. This is what happened:

Vernon was in his Safe Place, which now has a permanent opening in the forest surrounding it. He can see the hill leading up to Newgrange. The Goddess came to his Sanctuary and floated just to the left of him. She "gave" the history to him, as a soundless, singular understanding:

A huge ring of standing stones was erected on the Island of Orkney which had much masculine energy. Newgrange was built to create balance: the feminine of Newgrange to the masculine of that ring, called Brodgar. After Newgrange was built, however, the people realized that Brodgar was too far away to balance the Mound's huge, utterly feminine energy. The builders of Newgrange had built it "too well;" it had become more powerful than they had intended. They had to keep the feminine energy balanced by the nature of their ceremony, which they did. Over time, however, the ceremony became frozen in ritual and the understanding of the deeper purpose of the ceremony was lost. With the purpose of the ceremony lost, the ceremony itself was soon abandoned. Without purpose or ceremony to harness it, the power of the Mound became unusable. People's focus went elsewhere and they eventually left. Newgrange lay deserted.

After much time there were people who came back. The feminine power was still strong there at the Mound. The new people felt it, though they had no knowledge of the old ceremony. They did, however, have a deep understanding of the necessary balance between male and female forces. In order to achieve that balance they barred its entrance with massive stones to disrupt the power, and erected the phallic stones in front of the opening to divide and redirect it.

This work had taken a long time. Locating, hauling and carving the stones become part of the new people's culture and ceremony at the Mound. Even today, the new stones break up the Mound's surging power, balancing it and dispersing it through the landscape.

Vernon says that the "Shadow People" are reduced in number. Only a representative group now remains. He could see an empty spot in their group and asked about that. They replied, in a soundless passing of information, that they are waiting for it to be filled. Then Vernon said to them, *"I'll fill it when we go back"*. They are waiting for him. They are waiting for his return, when he will finish something interrupted so very long ago.

4/2/05

Quietly musing to himself in the warmth of our morning bed, Vernon asked, *"Why?"* Why this business of him needing to be at spot X in location Y? The answer floated back: *"It needs acknowledgment. It's just a tourist attraction now, an historical building. It needs acknowledgment."* The Mound and Ireland need him to be there to begin a re-awakening of the sacred power of Newgrange.

5/24/05

At Vernon's request, we set up a Past Life Experience session, using a permissive induction to initiate it. He entered a trance deeply and easily, going to a time previous to the time when he was the New Shaman. This is a verbatim transcript of what he reported:

"The Mound is new. The grass is just starting to grow back from its construction. The sun is warm…curbstones are not in place yet."

I asked him to describe his feet and then his arms, a common technique in Past Life work, to anchor the traveler's body in a time and place. He described his feet as *"deep tan ...wide... heavy sandals,"* i.e. completely unlike his own which are narrow, white and always in shoes and socks. He described his arms as: *"bare... bracelets...strong, short-fingered hands"*...again, completely unlike his own.

K: What is your role here?

V: *"I'm a tribal elder... one of several trained from childhood to be aware of the turn of the seasons... To be aware of the connection we still have to the Earth...the Mother... which is why we have built this memorial (sic.). We've gathered together to acknowledge the presence of the Mother---already it is strong... We are One. As the children leave home, they need a focal point, a reminder of their origins from the Mother. We have all chipped stone... carried... planned...we are all still One... and not alone."*

K: Is there a message from this experience?

V: *"Mother is tired. Some seek to return. There will be others. His* (Vernon's) *acknowledgment of the Mother will help to restore Her health and well-being. He* (Vernon) *will know more about what to do. We will tell him. As he learns, he will know."* (This rather odd separation of the current Vernon from the man he was at Newgrange is common in the Past Life Experience, especially when the knowledge is important for the present-time person to learn.)

After he awoke, he said, *"I've never felt anything like that before! They'd just finished it. The spiral stone (which now lies across the entry) was in a different place. It was moved in later. The sheer power of love and warmth coming out of the entry was like standing in a warm river."*

05/30/05

Vernon and I had been attending a ten-week study stemming from the Native American Medicine Wheel teachings. The event for one of the classes was "trance-dancing"—opening the psyche to accept a totem animal's energy and meaning within music and dance. All thirty or so in the class wore blindfolds, to keep our experiences private and to help the "inner view" remain untouched by what another person might be doing. I was off in the ocean as a dolphin, but Vernon had a very different experience. There was no animal for him. He reported riding the *"wind between the stars,"* traveling among the planets. He said he eventually came home to Earth, realizing he had been channeling the Energy of Creation. He did not know what to think about that.

During a later Alpha-Reiki treatment, Vernon requested another visit to Newgrange. He said later, *"I was standing just inside, looking out. The energy roars like a river. I saw the same elder outside who was there before."* (This was the elder he had been prior to this experience, now already an ancestor.) He said, *"The energy is pouring out of the opening."* Being within this energy *"allows us the ability to be beyond the pettiness that surrounds us."*

What is a Moon Ceremony?

In the Pagan traditions of the West, especially in the WICCA tradition, ceremonies are often held at the full moon. The phases of the moon are important "circuits" from which we draw our energy for the work we do. Unlike the festivals, moon ceremonies are "working" ceremonies. Requests are made for finding love, increasing money, finding lost animals, help with projects, bounty of crops and other needed things. Different types of work, or for different stages in bigger projects, are best done at different phases of the moon. The full moon is considered the strongest time for healings.

Moon Ceremonies are perhaps viewed as the most secretive of the things WICCANS do. This is because doing the work requires a thorough knowledge of energy work, and a close relationship among the participants, with the ability to blend their energy in harmony. A long time of adjustments and understandings is required before a group reaches its potential strength in the work it does. Groups tend not to advertise or allow non-initiates to observe, as it disrupts that energetic harmony.

A "Ma" chant (mentioned in the text) begins with a group singing the syllable in a low and quiet tone, each one starting and stopping at will, repeatedly. Each singer begins the next "Ma" slightly louder and in a higher tone. This increases until a wall, or cone, of sound and energy is built around a person or item to be charged. At a mutually "felt" signal, the group stops suddenly and lets the silence reverberate with the energy of the "Ma", directing this energy into the person or item for whom the chant is sung.

An Ohm chant, much gentler in nature, is sung much as the Ma chant, but without the buildup in volume and pitch. Also, there is no sudden ending.

July 2005 Moon Ceremony

Vernon himself writes:

"On Sat., July 23, '05, my wife, Kate, and I attended a full moon healing ritual. I asked for the four people in the circle to send healing energy to my eyes, as I have been having trouble focusing. The group circled around me and concentrated on me while Kate led us all in a meditation. I went into an alpha state during which I opened to receive the energy being sent to me. I pictured an image of the Goddess standing before me adding Her healing energy to that of the circle around me. As the energy continued to come to me I saw a circle of blue light expand around me. As the light expanded to include the Goddess, I saw figures standing behind Her, stretching back to the base of a small hill. On top of the hill was Newgrange. Even though it was after sunset, the quartz facing around the passage way was glowing. The entrance itself was very black. The standing stones were also visible. The Goddess, the figures, and I were all in a line with the opening, and I could feel energy flowing from it.

The figures were dressed in what seemed to be leather clothing of several different designs. The designs of the clothing appeared to be older or more primitive as they got closer to Newgrange, as if they were going back in time. I felt they were all focused on me, adding their energy to that of the Goddess and to the group around me. I had a strong feeling of belonging with them, and with the

Goddess. I now understand that the Goddess and the other figures were the ever-renewed priests and priestesses of Newgrange.

After the session ended our friend Shirley said that she had seen light blue glow around my head. I felt very light and somewhat unbalanced. The next morning my left side felt lighter though I was still a little off balance. My eyes have shown a great improvement both in focus and in the blind spot being smaller.

My intent was to receive healing energy from strong people who were able to work together. I also grounded and centered and had intended to add their energy with the image of the Goddess. The appearance of the other figures and of Newgrange was an unplanned surprise."

*****

Aug. 2005 Moon Ceremony

Vernon writes:

"As the people gathered around me, Kate started me on my journey to Newgrange. The purpose of the journey was to help in a healing that the people were going to do for me. My first view of Newgrange was from a distance. I then got closer to the base of the hill Newgrange is located on; then I was closer again. I was closer again, directly in line with the entrance passage. The standing stones had not been put up yet and the curbstone with the spirals on it was also not in place. For the first time I was among the people gathered there, instead of standing off watching them. They were so close I could smell the leather of their clothes and feel the heat from their bodies. They had left an avenue between the passage entrance and me.

I could feel the people in the real Circle around me hold their hands toward me. I also saw the ones at Newgrange doing the same thing. As the "Ma" chant started, the people in the vision did the same. A warm flow of energy like a warm wind started to blow over me as the energy from our friends' hands poured over me. As the "Ma" chant increased, so did the strength of the energy from the passage and from the hands. Then the peak of the chant was reached and the flow ended. For a moment I stayed with the group at Newgrange, a strong, warm and friendly group of comrades that seemed to reach back thru the mist of time. They are still waiting.

The energy of the Moon Ceremony group was different this time. The first time the energy was strong and rather raw. It hit and filled me as was needed, as if I was empty. This time it was just as strong but it was more gentle, not as raw and in your face. As from the first time, I have felt a great improvement in my condition."

*****

Sept. 2005 Moon Ceremony

Vernon writes:

"At this moon ceremony, the group of 6 again raised energy to help in my healing from my stroke. Kate induced a light alpha condition, and suggested that if I wished I could go to a place of my choosing where I could receive a healing. Once again, I traveled to Newgrange. This time, instead of going first to my Safe Place from which I can view Newgrange, I went directly in line with the entrance. Gathered around me were the people that have become more and more real to me. They were standing so close I could smell the leather of their clothing and for the first time, I had a sense of sound from them. It was the low sound of a quiet crowd, and the sound of their clothing. Standing at my left shoulder was the one person who is in all of my journeys. He has come before, and I realized who he was: he is my guide, who came to me years ago.

My friends in the Circle were standing in end of daylight. As my Moon healing group joined hands around me, the light faded until it was very dark. The healers began an "Ohm" chant, joined by the Newgrange group. A light grew at the entrance to the passageway. As the "Ohm" chant grew in volume, so did the light, until it was a ball surrounding us all. The energy coming to me from the light and my moon group was so strong I had trouble breathing. I grew hot and began to shake.

The chant ended and the light faded, taking the Newgrange group with it. The last figure to go was the one that has become familiar, my guide. As I moved out of trance and back to the room, I felt weak and had trouble focusing my eyes.

The moon group also reported being affected by the energy. We all sat quietly, grounding ourselves for quite a while.

The results of the work became apparent in two days. My eyes were again improved; the blind spot was smaller and focus sharper. The numb feeling in my left side was reduced until it is now about 60% gone. My left leg is now almost clear, with stiffness only in my knee. For the first time in a year, I was able to jog, and to split firewood.

Each time it is easier and faster to go to Newgrange. The energy from my moon group gets stronger, and the results faster, as we work together on this project.

I feel that this is because I am working with a practiced, dedicated group. Also, I am assisting with their work. I also feel it is, in part, due to my being called to return to Newgrange. The group at Newgrange is helping the work."

*****

The Journal...

10/28/05

At Vernon's request, he and I did a guided Past Life Experience. He went first to his Safe Place, where there is now a path leading up to Newgrange. I gave him the suggestion to go to the "most important time" for him to be there. I asked him to describe himself. He began to walk on the path, noting his feet were large and that he had sandals on. He was male, and wearing a leather vest with crude pants and a leather belt. He had a bronze ax on his left side. His hands and arms were hairy, with short fingers. His hair was long, his cheekbones high, with deep eyes. He wore a bronze circlet on his head. There were others there. He spoke of his experience:

It is time to renew the Union with the Gods. It is my time to do the Calling. The other people are in pairs, lighting the purification fires on the path and setting the banquet tables. They are getting ready to acknowledge Deity and the Balance. My role is to acknowledge ourselves as representatives of Deity on earth. I am alone outside; my partner is coming from the Passageway. I have come first to prepare the way. I can smell warm forest smells. The sun is going down; the moon is cresting full. I've done this before.

K: Looking around you, tell me about it.

V: *The moon comes up. It is so bright ... it casts shadows. My partner comes toward me, walking on my shadow. She stands by my side and we acknowledge our balance in Union with the Earth and with the Gods. All comes from Creator. Energy flows warm from the Entrance of the Womb.*

I see all who have gone before…have done this in the past and in the future. I see us in both places. The togetherness of All lasts through the night 'til sunrise. As the sun rises, casting new shadows, we enter back into the world. The Power of the Energy—the Love—is there till we meet again.

K: Is this woman your life partner?

V: *More often than not she is, as time went by.*

K: When you go there in the near future, is the timing, or the ceremony itself, critical?

V: *It is the Intent. The time I'm in, and the time to come, when it will be done again…Our presence will complete the Cycle. The High Priestess will once again stand by my side. The trees are gone, the stones are placed there to control the Energy. The Love was too strong, though, and it has failed. It's been too long since the last Ceremony!* (Vernon is stating that the stones have not been able to contain the energy of Love from the Mound, and that he fears that the time since the last ceremony is so long that the ceremony has weakened. He refers to both the long-ago time he is experiencing in trance, and the time that he, Vernon, will be there.)

46

K: Are the Shadow People with you at Newgrange in 2006?

V: *They are gone… One will remain, representing the others.*

K: What is needed?

V: *Renewal of the Union of Shaman and Priestess… renewal of the Balance.*

Upon awakening, Vernon noted that the Newgrange he was seeing had no standing stones, nor curbstones. He was there before they were put into position. He was also aware that Newgrange was lunar, as well as solar.

*****

The Question

What is Vernon supposed to do once he gets there?

Dec. 21, '05, Vernon writes:

"*Having just spent 15 min. on the treadmill and with another 15 to go, I decided to try an experiment. Putting my hands on the guide rail I closed my eyes and began to synchronize my breathing with the rhythm of my walking, to relax as much as possible. When I was in sync, I crossed my fingers. This was the action that Kate and I had set up to put me into a light alpha state in my Sacred Place.*" (Notice that Vernon has shifted from calling it his Safe Place to his Sacred Place.)

I was sitting in my usual place under the large maple tree looking around the clearing. As I looked out of the opening in the trees I could see Newgrange shining on its hill across the river. For the first time I realized that the river was the River Boyne, the sacred river of Ireland. This time I did not go to Newgrange itself but just sat looking at it. Also, there were no other people with me. As usual, I was wondering what my role was to be. Gradually I began to understand what my first steps were to be. After entering the main chamber I will need to ground and center myself. Then I will open and merge myself with the energy that is in the chamber. I will then make a declaration of my intent, which is yet to be written. I will leave the chamber, walking out of the birth channel that is the passage, back into the world. After I leave the passage I will still have more to do, but that has yet to come clear to me. I will be with a tour group while I am doing all this, but it will still be valid, and I will do it in a non-disturbing way for the rest of the group."

*****

The Journal Continues...

Jan 2, '06

K: You can describe for me where you are.

V: *The air is cool...* (The walls inside are) *smooth—chip on one edge... It's light in the chamber...white sand on the floor... Making final inspection of chamber before capstone* (is placed on the top)... *Construction has gone well...no item left to chance... to be a very sacred spot... recognize power of Goddess and the One over all... the Source of our health, well-being... happiness... our protection.*

At my suggestion, he then moved forward in time, to one of the first Ceremonies after the completion of the site, and relates:

V: *It's cool...light reflecting down the tunnel...fills the chamber...all three...with light. I've been here all night...waiting for the light of the sun...I'm here to renew the bond...between the Lady and the Lord... and the People...feeling sheer love... almost too much!*

K: What is happening now?

V: *The people are waiting...I was chosen...go in...to carry the wishes and burdens of the village...to place them on the table near the wall.*

K: What did you put there on the table?

V: *Bundle…continuing representing the best the people had to offer… flowers, something with life…not easy to give.*

K: Looking into the chambers, what do you see?

V: *A small carving…on the right, the Goddess… on the left, the God…I'll leave the birth chamber and go past them… the love will follow me out… the people will hear the benediction and feel the energy… renew the land and renew the people."*

K: Tell me about the center, there on the floor.

V: *Sand from last year taken out…new layer laid…sparkling white sand…Directly under the top stone, in the center, is a spiral… a layer of different colored sand…wraps around and out…opens wider…Path of Life…Placed new each year…wears away in the coming and going of the year…births, weddings, remembrances for those who have passed on…It* (Newgrange) *needs the people as much as they need it…I take this bundle* (when I leave)…*each item returned to its owner, recharged.*

K: You can tell me more, if you will.

V: *Coming out…I am a representative of the people…not separate…no division… no disharmony…I am one…that is the message…the trials of living…we tend to forget…this is a reminder of who and what we are.*

Upon awakening, Vernon also pointed out that the bundle held items sent from other villages, too. Representatives of those villages were present and waiting outside. He also said that there were small smokeless candles in the chamber during the ceremony.

01/06

Vernon, a long time student of the Tarot, did a card reading for the coming year
	and
came to this conclusion:

"The numbers of the cards in this reading for 2006 totals 9. The numerological meaning of 9 is completion and birth. It seems I will have some sort of rebirth, of the spirit perhaps, when I enter the chamber and then exit thru the birth passage. I think that this will put me in the position to be able to acknowledge the power of Newgrange. I will in some way again be a priest of New Grange, as I was at its building."

03/22/06:

We decided to do another Past Life Regression to gather information about this other man's death and its meaning to Vernon at this time. We used my office, and Vernon went quickly to his Safe Place, and, in deep trance, he agreed to meet this man and hear the purpose of his contacting Vernon. It went like this:

K: Are you inside or outside?

V: *Outside….a group of us….at sunrise.*

K: Is everyone there who needs to be there?

V: *Yes…No…it's not time for the villagers to be there.*

K: Who is there?

V: *Old Shaman… and the ones who are training.*

K: Describe the atmosphere.

V: *Familiar…the ritual is comforting…*

K: What is your role?

V: *I am the oldest trainee… I am sick…*

K: Describe your sickness.

V: *Winter was hard… it hurts to breathe… One full moon… don't cough much anymore… fever… the Old Priest is dying… I was to enter the chamber and be blessed by the gods…and be reborn to take his place…I don't know if I can… I have to walk in…*

K: Can you walk?

V: *No... can't walk... I was helped by the younger ones... it's almost sunrise... fog is going back to the river... Villagers have come to the base of the hill... I have to walk from where I am... to the entrance... I can't... Others... waiting... I can feel the hope and energy from them... the Old Shaman is waiting... He can't walk (for me)* (V. pointed to himself indicating himself.)

K: How are you feeling?

V: *Close to death... physical...*

K: How are the others feeling?

V: *Fear... this is a period of decline... there have been other signs... strangers on the shore... failures of the crops... young don't live... they feel it's a turn...*

K: Look now and see yourself, as you will be in 2006. This one needs to know something to complete your walk for you.

V: *Everything he's gone through... has been to teach him the truth of Spirit... Enter the chamber and finish the rebirth... connect once again with the line of priests... till we emerge and finish the benediction... the blessing of the land and the people... this is part of the rebirth... of Spirit... not only here, but worldwide... others are doing it, too... it's almost time... for separation... of those who walk in Spirit... of whatever name... it's happening in other spiritual paths... as the sun*

53

comes up over the river... *Spirit will live in the hearts of the people... the Wheel turns again...*

K: Can you tell us about the Ceremony?

V: *Your bundle is a good idea* (I had decided to carry a bundle to the Mound, based upon his description of the ancient bundles)...*the Priestess goes first,* (into and out of the chamber)... *don't doubt... the blessing is simple... it will come gradually and be in place... when you both come back... have no choice but to teach...* (Some) *will simply go away... follow their own paths... others will learn...*

Thus, with Vernon tired, we ended the session. He told me upon awakening that there were no stones across the entrance, and no standing stones visible during this time.

Vernon wrote of the same experience:

"My question at the last Tarot class of March was, 'What is my purpose for being called to Newgrange?' I know I have to do a ritual of some kind there, but why and what shape it should take was still pretty hazy. The Tarot teacher, Bonnie O., said that the cards indicated that someone important had died young at Newgrange, and that the death was related to the purpose. This became very clear during the next regression that Kate took me on:

54

On this journey I realized that I had become very ill over a very hard winter. There was something wrong with my breathing and I felt (in the chair) *like I had to cough. I had been carried by others to a spot in line with the passage to the interior of the mound. It just before sunrise and the old priest was standing by my side. It was time for me to take my place as the New Priest of Newgrange. All I had to do was walk into the center chamber of the mound in time to stand in the light beam as it came down the passageway. I was then to walk out of the mound, being reborn in the service of the Great Goddess, and of the people. To complete the ritual, I was to acknowledge my position and give a blessing from the Goddess to the people and the land. All I had to do was stand and walk, but I was too ill to do so. The next student in line of succession was chosen to take my place. So, as the people came up the hill through the mist off the river, and as the sun rose and lit the roof box, another took the position of High Priest of Newgrange, and my line was broken.*

I now understand that I must enter the chamber and, even though it is not the Equinox, I can still stand in line with the roof box and open to the spirit of the Mother, walk out of the passage as a Priest of Newgrange, and finish the blessing from so long ago.

One morning, shortly after this regression, I was thinking about the ritual of the blessing. It came to me that this was the time and place to initiate Kate to 3rd degree Priestess as both High Priestess in Wicca, and as a High Priestess of Newgrange."

The Journal...

04/09/06

We are coming close to our time to return to Ireland. I have had a Tarot card reading about my own role there. The cards read, essentially, that I am to receive a great message there, and that life will be changed as I incorporate that message into my life.

It is recently that others have asked me, "Is Vernon planning to return from this trip?" I, too, have felt the breeze of that question on the back of my neck, as he has not made any plans for our summer. In March he did a Tarot card reading, in which both the Tower and Death cards presented. The reading had to do with the death of a man (perhaps the Shaman himself), long ago at Newgrange, however, and not Vernon in this lifetime.

*****

The Second Visit to Newgrange

2006

Our second trip to Newgrange was planned very differently from the first. Vernon and I went alone so we could be very flexible about our time. Vernon's stroke had left him easily fatigued, less able to hike the streets and by-ways. He also still became anxious when he was confused or unsure of his surroundings. We planned this trip simply: we would spend our two weeks in one B&B in Dublin with maps at hand. We would take day trips out of town to see the sights, and return each night to a familiar room. Newgrange is close to Dublin, a bus-ride away. We also hired a driver who took us to the places that buses don't go. We planned one overnight to a place called Power's Court, an amazing great house with a formal garden, well worth the extra night's fee (we kept our B&B, so we didn't have to pack up while we were gone.)

We had our driver take us to Newgrange, in part to free us from the bus schedule and in part because he had never been to see it. He had by then become a most enthusiastic participant in our excursions. The day was overcast and rather chilly. The wind blew and blew, but the Visitor's Center was warm and we had our focus. We spent considerable time at the mound, once we got there. We walked around the front of the mound, greeting the standing stones like old friends. We took the tour and entered the Chamber. In short, we were able to do our work as best we could in the wind and with the tourists around us. Oddly, and to our relief, we were mostly ignored and we were able to do all we had come to do.

57

Vernon writes of his experience at Newgrange:

"Kate and I walked up from the Visitor's Center at Bru na Boine to the standing stone that is just stage left of the passage into the Mound itself. The day was cold and cloudy. The wind blew at gale force strength and it was even a little hard to stand. We tried to lay a magical cord circle out but the wind was so strong that we had a hard time keeping it on the ground, much less to get it to lie in a circle. We finally did get it to spread out enough that we could stand in it and decided that, with our intent, it would be enough. Since our friends at home had already charged the cord, casting a formal circle was not necessary. We did, however, place a protective warding around us to divert any unwanted attention from the other visitors.

With the cord down, I initiated Kate to 3rd degree in a short ritual. We asked the guardians of the quarters, the elements and the Lady and Lord to witness us. Then, Kate had me put my hands on the stone (to connect with the energy of the Mound) *while she stood behind me. I relaxed and centered myself, focusing on the reason I was there. As Kate stood behind me, I crossed my fingers, slipped into a light alpha state and prepared myself for my journey into the chamber. I could hear Kate chanting behind me. As I gathered energy from the stone, the outside energy of the other people faded away. Several times I saw people glance in our direction, lose interest and look away. I felt the Shadow People, who have always been with me in my regressions, coming up the hill below us. Staying in a light alpha state, we walked to where the tour guide was forming a small group. After a short wait, we crossed the stairs and entered the passage into Newgrange.*

As I entered the passage, a strange mixture of peace and excitement filled me. There was none of the tension I normally have when I enter an enclosed space as low and narrow as this passage is. I was aware of the tourists around me but they were of no real importance to me. Pressured by the tour guide, I was not able to take the time I would have liked, but even as I hurried I felt at home. I bowed my head in the low spots and, and in the narrow places where the huge stone slabs hug together I turned my body to slip through in a natural, familiar way. The passage was warm and welcoming. I knew it had been waiting.

Entering the central chamber, I saw Kate against the far wall, opposite the passage at the location we had talked about. If it had been the proper time, at the solstice, I would be standing where the light from the sun would rest on me and bless me when it entered the chamber. Our guide was determined, however, and I had to stand to one side as she turned on the light that simulates the sun's beam. As the guide talked I turned slightly and I let her presence, and the presence of the others, fall away, until I was alone with the Spirit of the Creator. My mind and body filled with peace and love. I knew that I was again on the journey I had begun so many, many years ago.

Uncounted life times ago, the Old Shaman was dying. He knew that he had little time to train the one that was to replace him. I was the one he had chosen at the last solstice, but it had been a hard winter and I had fallen sick. All I had to do to

59

complete the ritual was walk into the chamber alone, stand in the beam of light to receive the blessing of the Creator, and walk out again to receive the blessing of rebirth by the Mother. I was then to give the blessing to the people and the land. I was too sick to do this. I was unable to stand and walk, and another was chosen in my place. I died shortly after. Now, after all the life times I have lived, I had arrived again at Newgrange. I had arrived as a Priest, trained, healthy, and ready. This time, I was able to complete my task. I accepted the blessing of the sun.

The guide, ever on schedule, began moving us out, allowing little time for reflection. Exiting the chamber, Kate and I returned to "our" stone. She again took her position behind me, chanting softly. The wind still howled; I heard the voice of the gods. I sensed the Shadow People, now joined by all my teachers and guides, standing on the hillside with me. Facing Newgrange, standing in the warm river of love and strength that flows from the Mother, I raised my hands and thanked the gods for their love and blessings, and called to them to continue to bless the land and its people.

I finished, and a feeling of utter calm, love and peace filled me. For the first time in my life I understood the meaning of "closure." An ancient, open wound is healed; my initiation is complete. Now this part of my journey ends. I am free to walk forward on my path knowing that my guides, the Lady and the Lord and the Creator of All, walk by my side."

GV McC 6/06

*****

Kate writes of her experience of the same event:

Ancient Mother, I hear you calling!
Ancient Mother, I hear your song.
Ancient Mother, I hear your laughter.
Ancient Mother, I taste your tears.

This is the chant that ran non-stop through my mind as we arrived in Ireland. It ran and ran, through the first couple of days, and while in the car we hired to take us to Newgrange. I was keenly aware of Vernon's presence, and of our purpose there. I wanted to shepherd him, protect and surround him. He, however, was talking, looking, filming, and in general, acting very normal about it all. I had the bundle we had put together from totems and tokens from those at home wishing to have a touch of Newgrange. I held the cameras, the charged cord, and my purse. I felt burdened.

And the wind: It howled at us, ripping things out of my hands, whisking away any control I thought I had, laughing. Did I really need anything? No, but the ceremonialist in me was cantankerous and I wanted organization. Even that was stripped away as others strictly monitored our trip to, into, and out of Newgrange. Everything was in "hurry up" mode.

Happily, we missed the first group entrance to the chamber, giving us a little time for ourselves. Vernon and I stood behind a standing stone near the entrance, evading the others and hoping to find shelter from the wind. The wind whipped the cord away and blew my hair and my scarf into a twist around my face as I tried to maintain dignity. Laughing, pulling and laughing again, the wind became one with me as Vernon initiated me to my 3rd Degree. And, as his Priestess, I began his work. I chanted and the wind sucked my words away from me, sending them out to the Universe before I could hear them myself. With his hands on the stone, Vernon drew in its energy, warmth and silence. He focused himself, gathered himself, entering that place inside the mind where one can see and understand beyond the shiny surface of things.

My job was to be so simple: enter before him, guard him, and be sure he was safe. It became a monumental task in the wind, and with the guide's need for absolute obedience and punctuality. The chamber was much smaller than I had remembered and the passageway lower, more difficult to navigate. Once in, I found I had to resist an overwhelming urge to lie down on the floor. I realized that I belonged there. I have spent much time there. The air inside is still and quiet. It is easy to breathe inside there. The stones lean inward as if in conversation. What had we interrupted? I let the guide and the others slip away from my mind and quietly put the bundle on the floor behind me, near the wall. As the light shone down the passageway, I cast a protective shield around Vernon, asking the light to bend and surround him there.

The guide invited us to move around and view the three smaller chambers, and I realized her speech was over. I hadn't heard a word of it. Vernon stayed within his shield, and I moved the bundle to each of the three chambers, calling on the energy of each to bless all within the bundle.

Vernon preceded me out of the chamber, back into the wind. I paused on the stairs, to let him go to the stone alone. I could see him giving the blessing to the land. I followed him to the stone and supported his inner work. He turned back towards the Mound to give and receive a blessing. He had a relaxed air about him and I realized that, despite the wind and the temperature, this man who thrives only in the full heat of July was not cold. I knew Energy was at work with us.

May the sacred power of Newgrange, now blessed and recognized, flow unchecked from her deep Sacred Center to bless all Ireland with fertility of its people, its land, its creative spirit, and its will.   KB 6/06

*****

2008

The Ending

*****

Finishing the Work

This, we thought, was to be Vernon's last "visit" to Newgrange. We had returned home from Ireland, and life had folded in around us. We had already noticed that Vernon's Safe Place had changed. It now included standing stones and a central fire pit. This is what he wrote:

"The purpose of this last regression to Newgrange was to see if I had properly completed the ritual that I felt I had been trained for, but unable to do, so long ago. I felt that I had, but I needed to check.

I entered my sanctuary in the usual way, walking between the standing stones at the entrance into the circular clearing under the ancient trees. The central fire burned low and the stream spoke softly in the background. A soft carpet of leaves from the maple covered the ground. Looking to my left over the stream I could see Newgrange through an opening in the trees. Shining in the soft light of the summer sun, the mound dominated everything around it. The time was before the carved curbstone or the tall standing stones had been put in place.

From my place in the circle I willed myself to the path leading to the entrance of the mound. As I stood waiting I could hear the voice of the goddess whispering in the grass as the warmth of the love flowing from the passage welcomed me home.

Before me the figure of my guide, whom I have come to know was the old Shaman of Newgrange, took shape. At this point I could hear Kate's voice asking me who was present. While I knew that the people of the tribe were not there, the old Shaman answered Kate by saying, "We are all here." I understood this to mean that the complete line of Shamans was present, and they were standing around us.

I knew then that I had completed my journey and given the blessing to the land and the people in the right way. The old Shaman was satisfied.

Kate began to call me back to the present. I could hear her calling me back, and I didn't want to return. I was home and I wanted to stay. I found myself walking up the path to the entrance behind the old Shaman, when he turned and held up his hand. He shook his head and I knew that I could not stay. I had to return to our work, Kate's and mine.

I know that we, me as priest and Kate as my priestess, are of the line of Newgrange priestly ones, and that our work is to tell all who will listen of the love of the goddess and god as Newgrange was meant to do.

When I went into the session I thought that the call of Newgrange was now behind me, but I was wrong. The Mound and Ireland are my soul's home and will always call to my spirit."

*****

2008: The Leave-taking

Early in 2008, Vernon was diagnosed with colon cancer, which had spread to his lung. He realized that he had truly finished his life's purpose, and chose to take his Final Journey without chemicals, and with grace. He entered the Hospice service in the summer of that year.

07/2008

I asked my sister to proofread part of the manuscript of this book. My husband lay in a Hospice bed in the living room, deep into his Final Journey. I was writing as a way to keep myself strong. She was thunderstruck when she proofed the manuscript, and told me the following:

She realized it was she who either had been or was now holding the energy of the young man, the hunter who, by events beyond his desires, became the new priest. She had been chosen to take the Priesthood, when Vernon could not take it. But she had been a hunter, not of priestly material, and had had to give up her passion to accept the role. She was sad, angry and confined about the decision of that day. She knew she had done the very best she could, for there was no other way to go.

While reading the manuscript, she had had a vision of part of the death ceremony for the young man who had died: The young man had been her brother or cousin. She (as the new priest) was pulling his body in a small sledge around the center of the village, so that all could see that the boy had, indeed, died. The villagers were gently tossing small clods of earth at her legs as she pulled the sledge.

Some believe in "soul groups" who travel through lifetimes, changing roles and sexes as they go. They finally meet together in just the right way, time and circumstance to recognize one another and to accomplish the work they need to do. That explains Vernon and Sabra coming together in this lifetime, able to bless and forgive one another now, forever. Sabra went to Vernon, and the two "boys" forgave each other for that time, so very long ago. Vernon blessed her. They sat alone in the room a long time, talking.

I had become aware that some further inner work needed to be done surrounding the events at the fateful Solstice Ceremony so long ago. With his permission, Vernon traveled back one last time to his beloved Newgrange, this time as his modern self.

07/20/08

In trance: (Through the guidance of the induction, he has gone back to that Solstice morning as the modern man that he is. He is invisible to all, but able to see and hear, and to speak to the sick young man who had been himself long ago.)

K: Can you forgive this young man for being so ill?

V: *Yes.*

K: What do you tell him?

V: *The time will come…you'll finish your work. You'll get up and walk, deliver the blessing…that's your job to do…great joy and love and peace…that's yours to give…land will be blessed…all the lands you travel through…you'll be able to do this…*

K: Seeing the other man there…can you forgive him for being chosen?

V: *Yes… It's part of the training he* (the sick one) *did…to accept adversity…He can pass on the love and dedication to him.*

K: Can you forgive the Universe for this situation?
V: *Yes…* (sighs)

K: The old Shaman can see the modern you, now. He recognizes who you are. He has something to say to you now. You can hear him; hear what he tells you, and you can tell me about it.

V: *He says…my forgiveness of my replacement adds to my ability… to travel…to do this again…this has added to me…*

*****

Conclusions

*****

Putting It All Together

At any given moment, an array of possibilities is open to humans. Many choices are available to us every minute that, once decided upon, gradually develop into a series of actions that directs the course of our lives. These decisions create our history. Sometimes people make great decisions. Sometimes they make disastrous ones. More often than not, expediency rules, and choices get made to best fit a moment, an emotion, or another short-term issue. Sometimes the results of our choices play out for years or decades as they interweave with the choices of the others around us.

At Newgrange a great Shaman was faced with several poor choices as his intended and beloved successor lay dying at his feet. He chose to initiate a lesser man, one not prepared to shoulder the job. The old man knew what he was doing, knew it was the best that he could do, and knew he was ushering in the end of an era for his people.

The second-choice initiate understood his own predicament as well, and kept the secret of his shame as an "also-ran." He knew he was chosen by force. He knew he had not wanted the position and had not prepared himself for the job. He knew that he did not have his master's love. Unable to refuse, he took the job bravely. He ignored his vulnerability and in doing so, lay aside the hunting life he longed for.

What played out is this:

The soul of the beloved young man too ill to accept the initiation has, in succeeding lifetimes, lived a legacy of believing himself less than able to become all he can be in a lifetime. He has lived lives bounded by a pervasive fear of failing, and of disappointing others. He has lived his lives unsure of his capabilities, being overlooked or un-chosen, and always willing to step aside as someone else took the spotlight. His lives have been based on developing his skills and using them quietly, alone, without fanfare or reward. In this lifetime, if not in others, he also has had a history of problems with his legs.

The one who was chosen and initiated lived his life under a cloud, knowing he was not the Shaman's first choice. He has lived many lifetimes stepping up to fill positions for which he was not prepared, and wondering why his projects degraded under his leadership.

And the land? An important, if not critical, blessing was not given properly at a time when great changes were developing. Without a proper blessing, and without strong leadership, the people became unsure and fearful. The ceremonies became ritualized, and their deeper meanings forgotten. Changes in weather and population were met with uncertainty, and a culture succumbed to disintegration.

Different people in Ireland have come and gone across the face of Newgrange, feeling its power, yet uncertain of how to use it. Standing stones were brought in and placed around the structure to harness this power and redirect it. Different ceremonies were developed, as people will do, over time and generations. A link in the chain of its history and its people had broken, however. Eventually the people abandoned the site permanently. Newgrange sat alone and empty in the mists, conversing only with the occasional wanderer seeking shelter, and with the Ghosts, the Shadow People who waited there.

*****

Reconstructing Beliefs and Ceremonies

The following interpretations and reconstructions are based solely upon the recovered memory of V. McCoy, during Past Life Experience.

At best, these are fragments, hints of the deep beliefs held by the people of early Ireland. Together, they give some breath and form to what their world was like to them. It is neither the stones nor great monuments that can tell the inner tale of a people. Their dreams, their fears, or their hopes are not made of stone. To understand who they are, a person must listen to their stories, their beliefs, or their way of seeing the world. Walk with them through their ceremonies, notice how they think about birth and death. These stories are lost when a culture vanishes with no written record.

If you can imagine that a person can remember things that have not happened in his lifetime, and if you can believe that such a person would travel across the world to pursue these memories and to finish what he believed had been left undone, then you can piece together the fragments presented in this book and gain a deeper understanding of the people of Newgrange, our spiritual ancestors, the builders of our Great Ceremonial Home.

1. Burial Practices and the Winter Solstice Ceremony

Though deeply and intrinsically tied to death and rebirth, Newgrange was more a ceremonial "completion" site, than a "burial" site. In the belief structure of the people who built it, life came from the Unknown. Conception occurred when life force was taken from the Unknown by the father and given to the child, in the womb of the mother, during the sexual union of two mortals. The child lived as long as possible, becoming an adult, growing old, and then dying. The people believed that the soul, or life force, was enmeshed within the body, unable to free itself on its own at death. Returning a soul to the Unknown was of paramount importance, for only when it was freed could the cycle continue: Souls entering the Unknown somehow freed souls to return to the Known, as newborns here on earth.

In order to liberate the soul from the body after death and return it to the Unknown, the people believed that a second sexual union was required. This second union needed to be non-mortal, a union between the Female Unknown (Earth) and the Male Unknown (Sky or Universe). Bodies of the dead were prepared and stored for this union.

Among its other functions as a solar and lunar calendar, the people created Newgrange to be a great womb for the earth. The womb aspect was built with the intent that it would unite with the Sky once a year, thus providing safe passage for the souls of the dead, returning them to the Unknown. Newgrange (the Womb:

feminine, dark and cool) was pierced by the sun (the Shaft: masculine, bright and hot) on the Solstice to conceive and give rebirth into the Unknown to the souls of the dead.

The Solstice sun disentangled the life force from the body, freeing it to ride the light out into the Universe, back into the Unknown from where it had mysteriously come, thus "Completing" the Cycle of Life.

Bodies of the dead were prepared by specially trained women within the community. The bodies were held until the Winter Solstice. They were then laid in the side chambers of the Mound during the ceremony, to be later removed and buried elsewhere after the ceremony was finished. Details of this were not made available to Vernon, as they may not have been part of the Shaman's knowledge. Such things may have been knowledge closely kept by the women who performed those duties.

Ceremonies, especially the Winter Solstice, were festive affairs. People came from all over the area for socializing, fortune telling, trading, selling, feasting, finding mates, and catching up on news. Those who could not attend sent special items bundled in leather, to be blessed. Inside each bundle was also something alive, like a blossom from a plant (difficult to find in winter), possibly an egg or a cocoon, to symbolize continuing life. The bundles came from all around the area, and were carried into the chamber for consecration by the Shaman during the ceremony. They were later returned to their villages to spread the hope and the blessing of the Solstice.

Before the Winter Solstice Ceremony, fresh crystalline sand was brought in and spread on the floor of the chamber. A spiral of different colored sand, laid down to represent the Path of Life, opened from the center of the chamber onto the passage. This remained throughout the year, worn away by the feet of those coming and going about the many ceremonies.

Two small carvings graced the interior near the passage: A Goddess on the right, A God on the left.

During night ceremonies, and probably during the day as well, small, smokeless candles lit the inner chamber.

Blessings, omens, love and natural balance were major themes of the spiritual community there.

When a Shaman died, the people believed that his soul was freed from the body by the Solstice sun. They believed that some of it would then re-enter the body of the new Shaman, uniting their knowledge and powers.

2. Some Details of Other Ceremonies

1. Full Moon

The time of year of this full moon ceremony was unclear, though spring seems a natural time.

It was a festival to renew the bond between Deity and the People. It was a ceremony of balance, and a time to recognize the Gods and their role as their representatives on earth. It was a time for blessing couples, old and new. It was a feasting time, and a fire ceremony. Fires were laid along the path from the village to Newgrange. These were lit by the first of the pairs of people coming from the village to the Mound for blessing. Others brought food to place along the tables between the fires. People came in pairs, male and female, from the village to the Mound. The Shaman emerged from the Mound first, to prepare the way for the Priestess. The nature of the term "prepare" is not clear, but may have involved being sure the fires were alight, the food well placed, and all signs and omens proper for a blessing. It was a time of blessing and acknowledgment of the union of humanity and the Creation, the necessity for balance, and to honor the People as the mortal representation of the Creator Spirit in consort with the Earth.

Balance was a key factor for the people, then: Balance between Male and Female, among the seasons, between the earth and the heavens, between all opposing forces and desires. Love was the second key, a deep, abiding love that permeated all things. The people believed it was the sustaining force of the universe.

As Vernon wrote:

It is time to renew the Union with the Gods. It is my time to do the Calling. The other people are in pairs, lighting the purification fires on the path and setting the banquet tables. They are getting ready to acknowledge Deity and the Balance. I'm here to renew the bond...between the Lady and the Lord... and the People. My role is to acknowledge ourselves as representatives of Deity on earth. I am alone outside; my partner is coming from the Passageway. I have come (from the

Chamber) *first to prepare the way. I can smell warm forest smells. The sun is going down. The moon is cresting full. I've done this before.*

2. Acknowledgment of Death

This ceremonial piece involves the initial burial formality, soon after death and before the body is prepared for its wait until Winter Solstice:

A family member pulls the body, laid on a small sledge, around the center of the village, so that all could see that the person has, indeed, died. This would quell any thoughts, perhaps, that the person had simply left the village. There is a secondary effect of pulling the sledge: The family member becomes tired, and is perhaps more willing to "let go" of the deceased when this is over.

The villagers gently toss clods of earth at the legs and feet of the one pulling the sledge. This, perhaps, was an early expression of "grounding" that person, so that he or she might stay on the earth with the living, and not follow the dead.

*****

Healing

"In the way of Healers there are two purposes of the work. Sometimes the 'healer' is assisting the body itself to heal its physical ailments. Just as often, and probably more importantly, one helps the person 'heal' the inside place where conflicts, resentments, disappointments and sorrow reside. We create a healing environment and/or ceremony for someone dying because we want that person to be utterly cleared of misgivings and fears, yearnings for this place, or despair before they leave us. That is, we help them 'heal.' Often, those involved in performing or offering a healing ceremony of any type will also find themselves healed of just that with which they are helping the other."

(From: **The Mountain and the Shadow, A Pagan's Journey Into Death**, by Kate Bowditch, MA, Lulu Pub., 2010)

*****

The Healing at Newgrange

A great healing has taken place at Newgrange. A break in an ancient lineage has been restored and strengthened. A neglected blessing has now been given to the land and its people. Perhaps the Ghosts, the Shadow People, can rest content now. Perhaps something within Newgrange itself can now awaken from its long and deep slumber.

By becoming conscious of this ancient legacy in his current lifetime, and by returning to Newgrange, Vernon healed a series of old wounds. The land, and many lifetimes, were wounded by the events of that day. Deprived of a strong Shaman at a critical point in their history, the people weakened. Unable to meet the challenges of their time, they scattered, abandoning Newgrange and their way of life. Now, Vernon has returned as a Shaman, and has done shamanic work there. He blessed the land with his open and loving heart, acting as a lens for the powerful love flowing from Newgrange. He sent that love out across the grasses, across the River Boyne, to spread far and wide across the land. He has not taken the lineage of the second initiate away from the other man, but rather has infused that lineage with his own love and forgiveness. Those wounds are healed now. With the land deeply blessed in a "right" manner; with sadness, anger and fear suffused with love and healing, his work is done. This blessing is part of a new rising, a new era, for Newgrange and for all Ireland.

*****

The Shaman of Newgrange

By: Kate Bowditch, MA

The following short story illustrates some of the many possible ceremonial details surrounding Newgrange Mound, in Ireland, at the dawn of its use.

*****

The Shaman of Newgrange

In the night, the shadows wait for dawn. They lie deep in the village, blurring the edges of low, stone dwellings. Vendor's tables hunker near the walls, their goods covered and safe from the bitter winds up at the Great Mound. They, too, wait for dawn and the coming day's celebration. For this is the night before the dawn of the Day of Great Turning, the Winter Solstice. On this dawn the sun will rise at its northernmost point on the horizon, heralding longer days coming, and the hope and certainty of spring's return.

Inside stone huts, morning fires lick at the edges of darkness, as folk prepare food early for this day. Solstice is festive. The villagers are eager to climb the Mound, receive the Shaman's blessings, and to hear his readings for the coming year. They are eager, too, to return to their warm fires, to feast and trade from those tables, to tell their stories and display their marriageable young ones with hopes of future pairings. Shamans from other villages have already arrived, giving their totems to the Shaman of the Mound to be blessed in ceremony. They will take these items back to their villages, to bring the energy of the Great Mound into their own ceremonies at home. All things wait for dawn.

Up on the hill, inside the Great Mound, there is a different energy. The dead of the last year rest on shallow stone slabs in the three chambers around the interior. It has been a hard year; there are several. They have been prepared and held for this day. It is only at the Winter Solstice that the soul can leave the body, free to re-enter the Place Beyond, the Home, where they had been before their birth into this world.

Only during these five short days, and only at dawn, will the rising sun enter the light box above the passage door of the Great Mound. Reaching the interior back wall of the Mound's central chamber, this piercing shaft of light will illuminate the Great Womb of the Mother from the floor to its conical ceiling, high above. The souls of the dead will leap from their bodies. They will ride the light out through the light box to be born again to the sky, as they were born to this world years before.

The Shaman has sat with the bodies all night, seeing by the dim light of small, smokeless candles. He has sung to the bodies, friends all, as a mother sings to her unborn child. He has talked to them, getting them ready for sunrise. He is vaguely unsatisfied, though, as though something were missing. He knows he is not well, but it seems more than that. Adjusting his cloak stiffly against the cold of the chamber he remembers another Solstice of uncertainty long ago. He was a young man, then. He remembers how new he had been to the position of Shaman, performing this Solstice rite for the first time and for the Old Shaman himself. That had been a good winter, for the Old Shaman's body was the only one in the Chamber. He had extinguished the little candles and stepped outside into the early light, leaving the Birthing to the Mother. He did not handle the body after the Birthing. That is the work of the Priestess. As he stood before the villagers in the growing light that day, he had noticed shadows in the valley. Focusing, he had seen them; the Old Shaman had told him about them. They were the souls of the others who had passed, coming to greet the Old Shaman on his return. They had filled the valley below, waiting for their beloved leader.

The Shaman remembers his excitement at seeing them. He had turned to face the Mound just as the first shaft of the rising sun flashed and entered the Mound through the window. He remembered how it was as he had stood and waited. The Old Soul was liberated from its body and it had ridden out on the light. He had felt it. He had felt the Old Shaman's familiar presence wash over him, warming him and giving him courage to do the work of this life. He remembers how he had sucked in his breath as he realized that he was, at that moment, both the Old Shaman and the New Shaman. They had become, and perhaps always had been somehow, one. Would this be so at his own re-birthing, when he rode the light?

He wonders at all this remembering.

Shaking his head, he redirects his attention to the dawn before him. The work of the night has seemed heavy, heavier than usual, and he wonders about that. Things seem in order, and the night's work has unfolded in a good way. The chamber had been properly swept clean for the ceremony. Bright crystalline sand had been laid down inside, helping spread the light of the little candles. Sand of a different color spiraled from the center of the chamber, opening to the passageway. This spiral will be worn away by the comings and goings in the Mound throughout the rest of the year. He has always liked that idea. The Shaman smiles, though feeling somehow separate from it all this year. He wonders at that, too.

He gazes fondly at two statues, the Goddess, and the God, guarding the opening from the chamber to the passageway. They mark the transition from the inner work of himself, alone in the chamber, to the outer work of the people and the land. They have always been there, those statues, and have long been participants in his silent conversations. The earliest light of dawn has begun; the great stone slabs of the passage begin a subtle back-light to the statues. How many more times will he exit this chamber, passing through these forms? He appreciates their balance. Each is powerful, the male and female, and each essential. He enjoys this vital balance: summer and winter, death and birth, night and day. Winter Solstice has always made him a bit uneasy, with its extremes. What would happen if the sun simply continued on its way North? The statues silently remind him to remember the ceremony.

They seem to say, as they have so often before, "The ceremony maintains the balance, and, through you, balance remains." He shivers. The Priestess will be arriving soon. She is leading a procession of villagers up the hill, and will greet him at sunrise. Relief loosens his shoulders as he is reminded of the balance that he and the Priestess embody. He has been fortunate in their work together over the years.

He smiles at the thought of her, realizing how serious he has been tonight. If he and she are the balance, so too are the Inside and the Outside, Villagers and Priestly ones, God and Goddess, Winter and Summer. All is Balance. All is Balance. The ceremony acknowledges that balance, and celebrates its perfection as shown by the returning sun. Remembering how it was to be young those many years ago, he softly sighs.

He is combining two ceremonies today, and is not as sure of himself as he likes to be. It is unusual, combining two ceremonies into one. It had been his choice by necessity, and yet something still tugged at him. Today he will greet the man whom he will initiate and train to replace himself. He has moved this initiation ceremony up from the spring, for the Shaman knows deeply that he is dying. He knows it, and knows it will be a steady, undramatic death. Only by beginning immediately will he be able to train his replacement in the deepest secrets of the sacred work. He is concerned, however, for the young man, too, is ill. He does not seem to be getting better. Can this be an omen? He has seen other signs of concern: the young are not thriving and there have been reports of strangers arriving on the northern shores. Crops have not matured properly the last few years. This past year has been particularly hard.

Looking around the chamber to see that all is in place, the Shaman rises stiffly. He bends to snuff the little candles one by one. As each candle surrenders, the chamber wraps him gently in a cloak of darkness. The passage has grown a little brighter, beckoning him to come and greet the Initiate. With the last candle, he steps into the center of the chamber and says his last good bye to the dead.

Chanting quietly to himself, he walks the colored spiral from the center of the chamber to the opening of the passage. Carefully stepping between the God and the Goddess, he enters great slabs of stone lining the long passageway of the Mound. The slabs lean towards each other, narrowing the way as he walks and forcing him to keep his head low. Like a newborn, he finally turns, crouched, pushing one shoulder through at a time to step out between the flanks of the Mound to greet the dawn.

As he raises his staff to greet the day, his heart falls. The Initiate is sitting on the ground, unable to stand. This is worse than he knew. How does he greet such a man? Shuddering, he is afraid for his people for the first time. This omen cannot be ignored. He swallows his fear; he will have to bear it alone. Perhaps he can make it right by his strong will. Pulling himself as straight as his old body allows, he walks out towards the Initiate. Glaring at him fiercely, hoping to give him strength, he commands him, "Stand! Walk with me!"

The Initiate looks up at him, his face streaked with tears. His face and arms glisten with the sweat of his effort in the dank morning air. He can neither stand nor walk. The Shaman reads his face easily, hearing his thoughts: It had seemed so simple before—all he needed to do was walk into the chamber, but his body will not respond to his desires.

The Initiate's breath is shallow and hard, as his arms and legs shake beneath him. He cannot manifest all he that has worked for since his childhood. He cannot match his beloved Shaman's expectations of him. He, too, is dying. They look long at one another. The Shaman's thought is a promise, "Another time, young one, another time. We will do this another time." The message is sent and received silently. Looking up, the Shaman sees the Priestess arriving with the villagers. The sun will soon rise. There is no more time. He accepts the omen heavily. Life, and Ceremony, cannot wait.

Forcing himself, the Old Shaman slowly turns his head. His piercing eyes rest upon the oldest of the other young students. "Walk with me!" he commands. Not daring to look again at his favorite, he walks back toward the Mound with the young man whom he will initiate as Shaman of the Mother. They walk into the strength of the Mother, which flows out over the land like a warm wind from her great flanks. This is a strength given freely by the Mother, balanced by the ceremony of her children. The Shaman stops, allowing the Initiate to enter the Mound. The young man will wait alone in the dark of the Womb. When the Solstice sun rises to enter the light box, he will be born into his new role as Shaman of the Mother. This year it will be this young man who will bless the land and begin the new chapter.

The winter sun rises behind him, driving the Shaman's shadow before him. He feels the Priestess take her place beside him as her long soft shadow joins his.

Whatever the future may bring, they wait, balanced, for the future, and for the souls of the dead to ride the light and be reborn.

89

George Vernon McCoy

On August 18th, 2008, McCoy died quietly in his home.

He was surrounded, supported, and loved by many.

May he be welcome in the land of his ancestors.

Blessed be

*****

<u>Appendix</u>

The following short articles will prepare the reader for terms used in the body of this work.

*****

Hypnosis and Hypnotic Inductions

Hypnosis describes a state of the mind during deep relaxation and comfort. Some call it a trance state, and most of us experience this state at least once a day. This state is reached in daydreaming, in being on "auto-pilot" during routine work, or just before letting go of the day and falling asleep. In this state, the subconscious mind is active, unfettered by the worries and concerns of the conscious mind.

When creating this state as a purposeful act, the transition from the conscious mind to the subconscious mind is eased by an event or an action of some sort. One may gaze softly at a candle, drum to oneself, chant, rock back and forth, or listen to the soft suggestibility of the spoken word from another person. This spoken transition is called the "induction", as it "induces" the trance state by suggesting deeper and deeper relaxation and focus, thus eliminating the mind's tendency to flit from thought to thought when the body is still. The induction allows the client's conscious mind to rest, freeing the subconscious to express itself through words, pictures, and/or feelings.

Inductions can be long, up to fifteen minutes of quiet suggestions, or very short, depending upon the readiness of the client, and the confidence and skill of the hypnotist. One prominent hypnotist, Milton Erickson, reportedly could induce a deep trance with only a handshake and a way of gazing at the client.

The hypnotic quieting of the mind with focus to diminish distractions are often enough to allow healing, deep-felt knowledge or creative thought to occur. In the guided hypnotic state of Past Life Experience, this quiet allows the hypnotist to gently inquire of the client certain information about feelings, experiences, or knowledge that are held only in the subconscious mind. As there are no time constraints to the memory of the subconscious mind, the knowledge can come from any time period or location that the mind has experienced.

The Safe Place

From the dawn of time living things have sought ways to shelter themselves from predators. Some have made hard shells, others use coloration. Some burrow into the dirt. Humans have created many ways to protect themselves from many perceived predators, from the King over the mountains to bad weather. We all seek a safe place to rest, a place to drop our defenses and enjoy the life we have, even for one night.

One's personal "Safe Place" can be the home or any location where one feels protected from outside attack. In modern times, personal physical safety is fragile enough to recommend the very real construction of a "Panic Room" inside one's own home. The concept of the Safe Place in hypnosis is an expansion of that concept. It involves creating a place of safety in the mind, Our Safe Place.

The hypnotic Safe Place recognizes the other side of physical safety: emotional safety, where one is protected from the disdain, disapproval, or demands of others. Creating a Safe Place in the mind that is specific only to the viewer gives one a place so safe that one can act, think, and appear exactly as one wishes without fear of reproach or attack. This made up location can be so safe it can be created "out-doors," in an open park or wild place where no one ever comes without the creator's permission. It can also be in a wonderful room one has only dreamed of.

The purpose of building such a place during hypnotherapy work is to allow for retreat to it if the material of the therapy brings up emotions that are too difficult to bear all at once. Retreat to the Safe Place allows the client a moment's reprieve, without leaving the hypnotic state. Even when there is no therapeutic work to be done, spending time in one's Safe Place is wonderfully rejuvenating to the soul and calming to the nerves, providing a moment's vacation from the stresses and strains of everyday life.

What is the Past Life Experience?

What is the nature of this thing we call the Past Life Experience? What does it mean to mentally fly back in time, landing somewhere in a different country, a different time, frequently a different age or sex? With a reasonable guide (the counselor), one can explore a new persona, a new way of being, and freely apply what is learned from the experience to the current situation in the "here and now." But, one must ask, "What just happened?"

There are two major ways of approaching the Past Life Experience, each producing similar results during therapeutic hypnosis.

First Approach: This approach assumes the existence of a "soul" or other continuing force that is greater than this body and this life. When events are

94

remembered of a life previous to this one, the "Past Life Experience" is viewed as memories of a real experience. Based on the belief that the soul is timeless, this approach accepts the idea that it has had previous experiences in human form on this planet.

The memories of these experiences, though often fragmented, unpredictable or hard to identify (much like our memories of this life), are available to the subconscious mind. This approach postulates that, with assistance, a person can remember, re-experience, and learn things from an event that happened long ago as easily as one can from a recent event. The importance of this is the possibility of resolution of old issues which continue to influence the life being lived today.

 Second Approach: Not requiring a belief in the human soul, this approach holds that the subconscious mind, separate from the conscious mind, is infinitely creative. It creates its own reality throughout the life of the person, and acts with conviction upon the lessons learned and memories held, regardless of the outside, verifiable, reality of the incident. The "Past Life Experience" is seen as a creation made of bits and pieces of what has been learned about different times and places from movies, books, TV, fantasies, and experiences in this life. These are put together during hypnosis to create a persona within a particular setting long ago. This self-created persona then allows the traveler to sidestep the "now" and experience a way of being that is safe enough to learn from, but which is not viewed as "self."

This author's private practice and this book are based upon the perspective of the first approach.   *****

Two Rings of Stone

1. The Ring of Brodgar

Nestled into a circular ditch some 10'deep and 30'wide and 340' around, twenty-seven thin, tall stones stand silent guard over their thirty-three fallen brethren. To get to this place, one can go first to Inverness, Scotland, then north again to John o' Groats, or Caithness, mere dots on the map. A ferry takes the traveler northeast across the cold waters to the Orkney Isles, small islands that have seen both Norwegian and Scottish sovereignty over the historical centuries.

Once a teeming hub of Neolithic activity, the Orkneys are a banquet of ancient finds, from single stones, stones in relationship, to stones in rings. An entire stone village, Scara Brae, was discovered under the earth, and mounds similar to Newgrange, though smaller. Many of these finds are easily accessible to the traveler. The Ring of Brodgar, also spelled "Brogar", was begun some 2,500 years BCE. As with the many other sites of those years, the big sites were started, modified, added to, abandoned, re-used, and abandoned again. The purpose of the Ring is lost with those who built it, and the stones keep their secrets. The center of the Ring has never been excavated, so its use as a lunar observatory, meeting place, ancestor honoring, or political meeting hall has only been guessed at. Its power and mystery are palpable, however, and all visitors fall silent when visiting.

Recent archaeological exploration in 2008 will provide more information on this wonderful place and those who lived there.

I admit I was a little disappointed as I walked toward the Ring. The stones, though tall, are thin. Many are broken or have fallen. Somehow, it seemed small, and a little sad. Then I stepped inside. Time and space shifted. The stones stretched hugely over me; the center swept away, vast. The silence of mystery took me over. Regaining my balance, I stepped outside the Ring, and walked away. Looking back, I saw it again, small, hunched, and a little sad. Curious, I returned. Again, I was sucked into the time/space vortex that is the Ring of Brodgar, unexplainable and indescribable. I hope to return.

2. Big Horn Medicine Wheel

Large white stones rest in the dusty earth just south of the Montana/Wyoming border in the U.S., high in the Big Horn Mountains. They form a great circle some 80 feet across. Twenty-seven spokes made of stones radiate from a central cairn; five stone cairns adorn the outside rim. This is the Medicine Wheel, ancient in origin; built upon a bluff of original, unchanged earth-mantle stone.

Few come here, for the walk is long and hot up the dirt cut-away road from the ranger station below. The thirsty air sucked at our skin as my husband and I walked, grateful for the benches along the way. There are no trees here, and the wind and sun are unrelenting.

At last, as the road bent to the left, the Wheel revealed itself. We were struck with the need for silence, for deep respect. The Wheel hugs the ground, yet commands the center of a breathtaking view of the world in all directions. We walked the periphery of the Wheel in prayer, leaving a talisman on the fence with the many others.

The origin of the Medicine Wheel is forgotten, yet its ongoing power has called for continued ceremony by any who come to know it. The first time my husband and I visited, there were people in the central cairn holding ceremony. As I walked the fence-line, I could not stop the visions of Wheels, Mandalas, Kivas, Newgrange, the Ring of Brodgar, Galaxies, and Sacred Spirals spinning and interweaving their shapes and meanings in my mind. Healing takes place here, even now.

This Wheel is perhaps the southernmost of several Wheels that were built from here north into Canada. Across the vast river valley below and up onto Carter Mountain over one hundred miles away to the southwest, lie more white stones. These form a 65-foot arrow, pointing directly to the Wheel. Big Horn Medicine Wheel rests on a foundation of First Stone, stone that is essentially unchanged from when the continents were one landmass, some 65,000,000 or more years ago. There are few such places on earth where this stone is exposed. That this Wheel is here, drawing on the unfiltered power of ancient Earth-Stone, speaks to the awareness and knowing of those who built it, and to the awareness of all those who come here with open heart and open mind.

The Tarot

The use of cards with symbolic pictures on them, for divination, is an old practice that developed deep in medieval Europe or earlier. Their history is tenuous, most easily traced through the culture of the wandering Romani peoples, who were guardians of the ancient interpretations of the symbols.

In essence, the cards in the deck represent and illustrate the lessons and burdens, joys and trials of life. By concentrating upon a question, shuffling and laying out the cards, then reading them accurately, one can see a situation from different perspective. Seeing a situation in this way gives the reader a chance to make choices or adjustments to the way he or she is living, learn what is needed and progress.

In the last thirty years, there has been a blossoming of the use of the Tarot. A multiplicity of new symbols and deck forms, can now be easily found. It is also fairly easy to find professional readers, and to take classes in reading the cards for one's own sake.

The study of the Tarot is a natural part of the education of those interested in metaphysics, the history of medieval Europe, arcane knowledge of all types, or the study of the subconscious mind. It is also useful for those simply interested in seeing their life situations from a broader perspective, giving them more choices for action in their lives.

*****

Bibliography

Newgrange references:
Newgrange Speaks for Itself, Forty Carved Motifs, Jacqueline Ingalls Garnett, Trafford Pub., USA, 2005
Newgrange, Archaeology, Art and Legend, Michael J. O'Kelly, Thames and Hudson Pub., London, 1982
www.ancient-wisdom.co.uk/irelandnewgrange.htm
www.myguideireland.com
ww.newgrangeireland.comw
Travel in Ireland
www.Newgrange.com
www.mysteriousbritain.co.uk/republic-of-ireland/meath/featured-sites/newgrange.html
www.mythicalireland.com/cygnus/cygnus2.html
http://www.philipcoppens.com/newgrange.html

Other Neolthic Sites:
Orkney, 2003, Orkney Tourist Board: www.visitorkney.com
"Ring of Brodgar", by Wendy Griffin. *The Beltane Papers*, Issue 6, Winter/Spring, Pg. 25-26.

Reiki:
The Reiki Handbook, A Manual for Students and Therapists. Larry E. Arnold and Sandra K. Nevius, PSI Press Int'l., 1982.
Healing Reiki, Eleanor McKenzie, Ulysses Press, CA, 1999.
The Mountain and the Shadow, A Pagan's Journey Into Death, Kate Bowditch, MA, Lulu Pub., 2010

Tarot:
The World of the Tarot, Sergius Golowin, English Pub., 1988
Conversations and study with Tarot Master Bonnie Osenbach, Everett, WA

Hypnosis and Past Life Experience:
Hypnotic Realities, Milton H Erickson, Irvington Pub., NY, 1976
Many Lives, Many Masters, Brian Weiss, Ph.D., Simon and Shuster, NY, 1988
20-20 Insight, Advanced Theory and Practice of Hypnosis,
Kate Bowditch, MA, LMHC, Lulu Pub., 2008

Other:
The Mountain and the Shadow, A Pagan's Journey Into Death,
Kate Bowditch, MA, Lulu Pub., 2010
"The Big Horn Medicine Wheel" by Jay Ellis Ransom, Yellowstone Printing & Publishing, 1992
Star Spider Dancing, www.ewebtribe.com

www.ingramcontent.com/pod-product-compliance
Lightning Source LLC
Chambersburg PA
CBHW081236090426
42738CB00016B/3321